Car Accident Claims: What You Need To Know!

Car Accident Claims: What You Need To Know!

Abraham S. Ovadia

ISBN-13: 9781541309562
ISBN-10: 1541309561

Contents

Dedication

I want to thank my family and friends for all of their help. Being a lawyer involves a lot of long hours and stress if you are doing it right. Family and friends have kept me sane, helped me grow as a person, and kept me grounded.

Mom and Anthony: you always encouraged me to fight for the little guy, stand up for what is right, and never forget where we came from.

My wife and children: you make me realize that there is more to life than work. I'm a workaholic, but the few hours that I spend with you each day bring me peace.

Sergio: you were my first employee back when I was working out of my mom's apartment seven years ago. You worked just as hard as I did (sometimes harder!) to get the job done and help our clients get the money that they deserve.

Alvaro, Chris, and Dave: you guys are the pillars of my success. If it wasn't for each of you, I might still be working out of my mom's apartment or that cramped office on Second Avenue. Having you guys on my team is an honor and a privilege.

Disclaimer

This book contains general tips and suggestions and does not constitute legal advice. Your car accident claim is unique, and you should speak with a lawyer about your specific legal situation.

Feel free to contact my office if you need to hire a lawyer in regard to your personal injury claim or want to ask questions. If you already have a lawyer and have questions, then contact him or her.

Preface

I wrote this book to help educate people who have been injured in a car accident and don't have a clue about what will happen to them. If you have never been in an accident, then you may have no idea where to turn. You might see billboards, hear commercials on the TV and radio, and get advice from tow-truck drivers and recommendations from friends who "know somebody," and all of these sources are telling you they are the *best* place to turn to after a car accident. Hopefully, this book can help some of you.

Also, I intentionally made this book easy to read so that everyone can understand. There won't be any legal talk here. I'm a lawyer who likes to write and speak in plain English, so that everything is clear and straightforward.

Part One:

Ten Mistakes After A Car Accident

Mistake One: Failing to File a Police Report

It is important to *always* file a police report after an accident. The first and most important document that insurance companies will look at to determine who is at fault for the car accident is the police report.

The police report usually includes

- the names of everyone involved in the accident;
- the insurance company information for the vehicles;
- the names and contact information for independent witnesses, if any;
- a diagram of the car accident scene and roads;
- a detailed explanation of the accident; and
- the names of anyone who was given a traffic ticket.

In Florida, if you weren't listed in the police report, then there is a presumption that you were not in the car accident. Make sure your name gets included in the police report.

Don't be like Todd—always file a police report

I represented Todd, who had been in a car accident. Todd told me that Sam caused the accident and that Sam agreed to pay for the repairs to Todd's car. The damage was less than $500, and Todd didn't want to wait ten minutes for the police to come. Todd took Sam's contact information and went home. Todd called Sam multiple times to pay for the repairs, but Sam never picked up. It turns out that Sam called the police immediately after Todd left the scene of the accident and filed a police report. Sam told the police that Todd caused the accident, and the police report reflected that information because Todd wasn't there. Todd couldn't convince the insurance companies that he was tricked by Sam, and he had no proof to support his claim. Todd had to pay out of his own pocket to repair his own vehicle. To add insult to injury, Todd's insurance paid to fix Sam's car damage.

Don't be like Rafael—make sure you are listed on the police report

I represented Rafael, who told me that he was a passenger in a vehicle that was rear-ended. Rafael wasn't listed on the police report. Rafael claims that the police officer didn't approach him and never took his information. Rafael assumed that because he was not a driver, he didn't need to talk to the police officer. The insurance companies viewed Rafael's claim with a lot of suspicion because he wasn't listed on the police report. I was eventually able to get written statements from both drivers involved to confirm that Rafael was in the vehicle at the time of the accident, but it delayed the case and took a lot of extra work.

Mistake Two: Failing to See a Doctor Right Away

After a car accident, it is your responsibility to prove you were injured in the car accident. Many of my clients are injured after a car accident but are so busy getting their car repaired and paying bills that they don't make time to see a doctor. If you see a doctor right away, it will help show the insurance company that you had injuries from the accident, and you will have proof in the form of medical records and a medical diagnosis from your doctor.

If you are injured immediately after an accident but don't see a doctor for six weeks, the insurance company is possibly going to view your claim as bogus. The insurance companies don't care if you work two jobs, take care of a sick elderly relative, or are going through a rough patch in your life. They only care about evaluating your car accident injuries in the light least favorable to you so that they can offer you less money for your injuries.

If you take too long to see a doctor, the insurance company can claim that (1) you weren't injured from the accident, or (2) you got hurt from something else after the car accident, and you are pulling a fast one by claiming your pain is from the accident.

If you aren't bleeding, didn't bump your head on anything, and don't feel like you are going to die, then you may want to go to an urgent care clinic or a chiropractor's office instead of the emergency room at a hospital. The urgent care/chiropractic visit is usually no more than $300, whereas the average hospital visit can be $5,000 to $25,000. The urgent care/chiropractic clinic will be able to evaluate your injuries and let you know if your injuries require an emergency room visit.

Important Note

In Florida, you need to see a doctor (doctor of medicine [MD], doctor of osteopathic medicine [DO], doctor of chiropractic [DC], dentist), visit a hospital, or receive treatment from a paramedic within fourteen days if you want to have access to $10,000 in personal injury protection (PIP) no-fault benefits from your insurance company.

Don't be like Cliff—don't have huge gaps in treatment

I represented Cliff. He was involved in a car accident and went to a hospital immediately afterward, where he complained of neck and lower back pain. The hospital gave him a lot of muscle relaxers and a note to follow up with an orthopedist. Cliff took the muscle relaxers but never followed up with any doctors because he didn't know which ones took his health insurance. He called my office after seeing one of my billboards and told me that he had a lot of pain from the accident, but he didn't know which doctor to go to. I helped set him up with a doctor who took his insurance, but two months had lapsed between the car accident and his visit with this doctor. When it came time for the auto insurance to make an offer to settle Cliff's case, the insurance company took into consideration the two-month gap in treatment. Even though Cliff was finally able to see a doctor and get some treatment that made him feel better (he underwent two steroid injections), the auto insurance took the two-month gap into consideration when making him an offer.

Mistake Three: Failing to Tell the Doctor Where You Feel Pain

Going to the doctor within a few days of the accident isn't enough. Making sure that you don't have huge, unexplainable gaps in treatment isn't enough. You need to make sure that you tell the doctor *all* of the areas where you feel pain from the car accident. Then you need to make sure that the doctor actually writes all those areas down.

If you start to develop pain in a new area (i.e., your left elbow), then make sure you report that new area to your doctor the next time you see him or her. It could become important down the road.

Don't be like Lisa—tell your doctor where you feel pain

I represented Lisa for her car accident case. Lisa went to a chiropractor the same day as the accident. Lisa told the chiropractor that her neck and lower back felt like they were on fire. Lisa did not mention the pain in her right knee because she was so concerned with her neck and lower back pain. Oddly enough, Lisa did fill out paperwork with my office stating that her neck, lower back, and right knee were in pain. After eight weeks, Lisa's neck and lower back pain reduced significantly with the chiropractic care, and she began to notice the pain in her right knee a lot more. She told the chiropractor about the pain in her right knee, and he documented it in his medical notes.

Six months after the car accident, Lisa had surgery on her right knee because the pain had become really bad. My office sent a demand letter to the at-fault insurance company, asking it to pay for all of Lisa's medical bills, including the surgery. The insurance company fought with us about whether it should cover the surgery on Lisa's right knee because Lisa did not have any medical records that documented this pain until eight weeks after the car accident. The insurance company believed that the injury to Lisa's right knee was a result of playing soccer, not the accident. We were eventually able to get the insurance company to put money on the table for the knee surgery because we got all of Lisa's medical records from her primary care doctor for the five years before the car accident, which showed she never complained to a doctor about her right knee.

MISTAKE FOUR: DOWNPLAYING YOUR LEVEL OF PAIN WITH THE DOCTOR

The doctor treating you after a car accident is probably the most important person involved in your car accident case besides your lawyer. You need to tell your doctor what areas of your body hurt after the car accident and how much pain you have in each area. For example, if you rate your neck pain as a five out of ten, with ten being the worst level of pain, then you need to let your doctor know. Some clients are afraid to tell the doctor that they have pain at a high level, such as a ten out of ten, because they are worried the doctor will recommend an injection or surgery. The "tough-guy" clients oftentimes downplay their injuries because they don't want to appear weak, and some clients have a very high pain tolerance. The insurance companies look at your medical records when evaluating your claim. If you have pain that you would rate as a ten (i.e., extreme pain), but you tell your doctor that you'd rate the pain as a two (i.e., minimal pain), then the insurance company is going to assume that you weren't hurt. The medical records are the "proof" of your injuries. There is a presumption that you tell your doctor the truth about the pain that you are having, and the insurance companies base their settlement offers on what you tell your doctor.

Don't be like Bonnie—be honest about your level of pain

I represented Bonnie after she was in a car accident. Bonnie was on a bicycle and was hit by a utility truck. When I signed up Bonnie, I could tell she was more worried about medical bills than she was about her pain. Two weeks after her car accident, she told her doctor that she would rate her pain as a zero out of ten. After a conversation with Bonnie, she confided in me that she was worried about having a lot of unpaid medical bills, so she decided to tell her doctor that she didn't have pain so that her doctor would release her from care and stop treating her. In actuality, Bonnie was producing medical records that stated she was not injured from the accident. This eventually led to a smaller settlement.

Don't be like Jean—don't try to play the system

Jean was a difficult client who called my office weekly and complained on the phone about how she couldn't get out of bed on some days because of her pain from the car accident. When I requested Jean's medical records from her doctor, I was surprised to find out that she told the doctor that her pain was a three out of ten (minimal). She saw the doctor three times a week for four months, and at every visit, she rated the pain level at around a three. Some visits, Jean complained about no pain! Jean had magnetic resonance imaging (MRI) scans of her neck and back, which showed several herniated discs. Jean did not get injections or surgery. The insurance company made an offer to settle for a few thousand dollars based on the low level of pain that Jean reported to the doctor. Jean was either lying to me about how much pain she had or she was lying to the doctor about her pain. Either way, the insurance company had medical records from forty-eight doctor visits where she said she had minimal to no pain, and the insurance company made an offer to settle based on that information.

Mistake Five: Failing to Be Regularly Treated by Your Doctor

If you don't go to the doctor regularly after a car accident, the insurance company is going to assume that you aren't hurt. Your medical records are your "proof" that you are injured. The less you are treated, the less proof you have. If you are having pain after a car accident, then why wouldn't you seek regular treatment? If you feel like you can't get out of bed, then make sure you see your doctor. Those are the days that I want the doctor to document your pain level. If you only go to the doctor on the "good" days, then your medical notes will show you feeling "good."

Don't be like Paula—if you have pain, then seek treatment

I signed up two car accident cases the same day—Tina and Paula. Tina was in a car accident that resulted in $900 in property damage. Paula was in a car accident with $12,000 in property damage. When I signed up both cases, I thought Paula was going to have a bigger case based on the property damage. Tina found time to go to a doctor three times a week, she got MRI scans of the areas that were in pain, and she got a couple of steroid injections in her neck and lower back as recommended by her doctor. On the other hand, Paula also had a lot of pain after the car accident, but she didn't see her doctor regularly or get the MRI scans recommended by the doctor. Tina's case ultimately settled for a lot more money than Paula's case because Tina followed her doctor's orders and received regular treatment. Tina also had a lot less pain by the time her case settled because the steroid injections worked. Paula got a smaller settlement and still had to live with a lot of pain by the time we settled her case.

Tina had a win-win scenario: less pain and more money for her injuries.

Paula had a lose-lose scenario—she still had a lot of pain from the car accident and received less money for her injuries.

Mistake Six: Failing to Do What Your Doctor Tells You

MRI scans are the gold standard of proving your injuries after a car accident. If you don't get MRI scans after a car accident, then you are doing a terrible job of proving you were injured, and no insurance company is going to take your claim seriously. MRI scans are literally a picture of what is causing your pain. MRI scans produce zero radiation, and you just have to lie down in the machine for the procedure. If you are claustrophobic, they have "open" machines that produce decent-quality images and don't cause stress to claustrophobic patients. If a doctor recommends that you undergo MRI and you don't, then the insurance company is going to assume you aren't really injured.

If a doctor recommends injections or surgery, then you should consider the pros/cons with your doctor and even seek a second opinion if you are unsure. You should also consult with your lawyer when possible to discuss how it could affect your case.

Insurance company adjusters look at car accidents like this: if you are really and truly in pain after a car accident, then you will get the recommended injection or surgery. A lot of people will seek chiropractic treatment even if they aren't in pain. It feels great, and chiropractors will typically wait until a car accident case settles to collect on the bill. But only people who are in pain will get an injection or surgery. The insurance company adjusters try to separate the "imposters" who have little to no pain from the people who are truly living with pain after a car accident.

If you end up getting injections or surgery while your car accident case is pending, the insurance company is legally obligated to pay for those expenses and pay for your pain and suffering related to those procedures. When I talk with my clients, I tell them that they can have the auto insurance pay for the procedures now or to be prepared to pay for those expenses in a couple of years out of their own pocket. Once a case is settled, it can't be reopened.

Don't be like Jerry—listen to your doctors

I represented Jerry in her car accident. She went to the chiropractor and got MRI scans showing that she had four herniated discs in her neck. She complained about a lot of pain but refused to get surgery. Her doctor was one of the best surgeons in South Florida, but she was naturally scared of having surgery on her neck. She told me to settle her case because she wouldn't get injections or surgery. I prepared all her medical records and sent a demand letter. We got an offer of $10,000 to settle her case. Jerry ultimately changed her mind and got the surgery, and the insurance company wrote her a check for the full policy limits of $100,000. She felt a lot better after the surgery and walked away with money in her pocket to compensate her for the surgery.

Mistake Seven: Thinking the Insurance Adjuster Is Your Friend

The insurance company's adjuster is not your friend. The adjuster is not calling you to see how you are doing. The adjuster's job is to be nice to you so that you think that you don't need to hire a lawyer. If you think the adjuster is being nice to you, then you are more likely to accept a smaller settlement. Sometimes the adjuster will offer you money right away and try to get you to sign settlement paperwork before you can hire a lawyer. Don't take it. Consult with a lawyer first. The consultation will usually be free.

Insurance companies are a business and want to make a profit for their shareholders/investors. They are not nonprofits or charities. They don't just hand out bags of cash to people who are injured after a car accident. They do not make a profit by helping you. They don't make a profit by giving you a ton of cash without a fight. They make a profit by taking insurance premiums from customers and then paying as little as possible to settle claims.

Take a look at the second appendix section on settlement offers to see just how much insurance companies negotiate with lawyers. Can you imagine how much they would low-ball nonlawyers who don't do this for a living?

Don't be like Alexis and Paul—consult with a lawyer before accepting any money

I just finished representing two people—Alexis and Paul—who were in a car accident together. They were offered about $500 each to cover lost wages and out-of-pocket medical bills. They cashed the checks the same day but never signed anything with the insurance company. They told me that they originally felt like they were getting free money but quickly realized they had serious injuries. They found their way to my office, and I just settled their cases for $100,000 each. Remember, the adjusters are not your friends. The insurance adjuster almost saved $95,500 per case by short-changing Alexis and Paul. I can only imagine how many people take the $500, sign off on the settlement, and have to live with all the pain and no money!

Don't be like John—consult with a lawyer before accepting any money

I represented a ninety-year-old man named John on the west coast of Florida. He was in a bad car accident and took a lot of prescription drugs to deal with the pain. Three days after the accident, a pushy insurance adjuster showed up at his house and talked him into settling his case for $1,000 and signing paperwork. He ultimately had to get major surgery on his neck. I was able to get this settlement thrown out because John was ninety years old and heavily medicated when he signed the paperwork, but it still delayed his case by two years and created a lot of extra work.

Mistake Eight: Talking with the Insurance Adjuster without a Lawyer

The main reason that insurance company adjusters are calling you is so that they can gather information before you get a lawyer. The insurance company adjuster works for the insurance company, not for you. The adjuster is going to take as much information from you as possible so that the insurance company can use it against you when it comes time to pay money on your claim. Insurance adjusters aren't bad people, but their job is to make sure they save money for their employers.

If you get a call from an insurance company adjuster after an accident, then you can tell him or her that (1) you hired a lawyer and to direct all calls to your lawyer or (2) you will call the adjuster back when you have time. The last thing you want to do is say something (or forget to say something) that could hurt your chance at getting compensated fairly for your injuries. If the car accident is clearly not your fault (e.g., you were fully stopped at red light and rear-ended), then it is usually OK for you to resolve your property damage claim on your own. However, it is preferred that you don't discuss your injuries without your lawyer on the phone. Most car accident lawyers in the United States handle these cases on the basis of "no settlement, no legal fees," which means you pay the lawyer nothing if you don't receive a settlement.

I recommend that you call a lawyer while you are at the scene of the accident. Sometimes, lawyers will send someone to the scene of the accident to take photos and take statements from any witnesses on the scene. Finding skid marks is rare, but the lawyer's office can send someone to take photos of that as well.

Don't be like Steve—hire a lawyer before you talk with the insurance company

I represented Steve, who told the insurance adjuster over the phone that "he was fine" and "he didn't have any pain" about three days after he was in the accident. This call was recorded by the insurance adjuster with permission from Steve before I was hired. Steve eventually developed a lot of pain two weeks after the accident and had surgery on his lower back. The injuries shown on Steve's MRI scans revealed multiple herniated discs in his lower back. There is no doubt in my mind that Steve was injured from the accident, but because he told the adjuster on a recorded line that he didn't have any pain, it impacted the value of his case. Everyone knows that it can take a few days or weeks to develop pain after an accident, but Steve didn't want to file a lawsuit and go to trial. He walked away with a decent settlement from the insurance company, but it would have been better if he hadn't talked with the insurance company prior to hiring a lawyer.

Don't be like Stacy—don't piss everyone off with your bad temper

I represented Stacy after she was involved in a car accident. Stacy had a really bad temper. Stacy yelled at the police officer who wrote the police report. Stacy yelled at the insurance adjuster too. Stacy even yelled at me. But when she finally calmed down, I was able to figure out how the accident happened. If Stacy had called me from the scene of the accident, I would have been able to tell the police officer what really happened. If she hadn't pissed off everyone before hiring me, I might have been able to get this information to the insurance adjuster before everyone put Stacy at fault for the accident. I ended up filing a lawsuit on behalf of Stacy because I believed her side of the story.

Mistake Nine: Waiting Too Long to Hire a Lawyer

Hiring a lawyer early in your case is important. Most people hire a lawyer within a few days of the car accident. The lawyer will deal with a lot of headaches for you. The lawyer will also watch out for you and make sure you are getting the correct treatment. Some doctors have a reputation for telling everyone they need surgery. Some surgeons have a great bedside manner but are horrible in the operating room. Some surgeons are known to drink all night and then do surgery the next morning. I keep my clients away from those surgeons. People who hire a lawyer within a few days after an accident have a better experience after a car accident. Period.

Don't be like Pam—hire a lawyer immediately after a car accident

I represented Pam, who was involved in a head-on collision at forty miles per hour. There were two other people in the car with Pam. The other two people hired lawyers right away and settled for $50,000 each within six months of the car accident. Pam didn't want to hire a lawyer. She just wanted to "feel better" and didn't realize that the other people in the car had hired lawyers. Pam had $50,000 in PIP no-fault coverage from her New York car insurance company. She thought she could just keep using that insurance coverage to pay her doctor's bills. Pam was treated by a doctor who didn't know how to properly document her injuries. That doctor goes down in history as keeping the worst medical records I've ever seen! Eventually, Pam's insurance company cut off her PIP no-fault benefits and stopped paying her doctor bills. Because she was no longer able to see a doctor with her PIP no-fault insurance, Pam got angry and hired me—three years after her car accident. I got all of her medical records and sent a demand letter to the at-fault insurance company, and the company offered her a whopping $300 to settle her case. I filed a lawsuit immediately after receiving the insulting offer. Pam eventually took $3,000 to settle her case because we were a month away from going to trial, and Pam didn't want to go to trial. If she had hired me right after the accident, I could have helped Pam find some doctors who could have helped her get better, properly documented her injuries, and her settlement would have been more in line with those of the other people who were in the car with Pam.

MISTAKE TEN: NOT HIRING THE RIGHT LAWYER

Not all lawyers are the same. I know some lawyers who have never filed a lawsuit in their twenty-year careers. Other lawyers want to file a lawsuit in every case and take them to trial. Other lawyers want to push their clients to get surgery when they don't need it so that there will be a bigger settlement. The insurance companies know these lawyers too.

I think we all know that you don't want the lawyer who "settles" every case without filing a lawsuit. The insurance companies offer smaller settlements to such lawyers because they know that these lawyers get lost on their way to the courthouse.

At the same time, you don't want the lawyer who thinks every case is going to trial. Those lawyers often reject a lot of potential clients with moderate injuries because they only want to work on the "big" cases. The minute that you tell them you won't get surgery, such lawyers will drop your case. Also, many of my clients don't want to go to trial. It can take two years from the date you file a lawsuit before your case gets to trial. The insurance companies and their lawyers have the money to appeal any case if they want to, which can add another two years after the trial. Most of my clients want a fair settlement and want to move on with their lives.

My office handles a lot of different car accident cases, and we always fight for a fair settlement. Check out the second appendix on settlements to see just how hard we fight for our clients. If the insurance company gives my client a low-ball offer, then we can file a lawsuit. In my career, I've filed lawsuits in more than forty counties in Florida. In my first three years as a lawyer, I filed more than five thousand lawsuits.

Part Two:

What Your Car Accident Lawyer Does

Step One: Meeting the Client, Signing the Retainer, and Investigating

The first step for the lawyer's office is to sign up the client. Some lawyers require the client to go to the lawyer's office and sign up in the conference room. Other lawyers will send someone to meet with the client at the client's house or any location that is more convenient for the client. I understand that people are often very busy right after a car accident—being injured, getting a rental car, having to see multiple doctors, and still dealing with their regular day-to-day activities, such as picking up the kids and going to work.

Although I prefer seeing clients sign up at my office, I have signed up clients at the scene of the accident, in their hospital rooms, at the doctor's office, at a nearby Starbucks, and at the client's home. Nowadays, clients want everything immediately, and we try to keep up with that demand while still offering top-notch legal services. If the client doesn't come to the office to meet with the lawyer when the client signs up, then we will usually have the client do a telephone call with the lawyer within the first week to make sure the client's questions get answered.

The retainer agreement is a contract between the client and the law firm. It will tell you how much money the lawyer will charge. Most car accident lawyers in the United States handle car accident cases on the basis of "no settlement, no legal fees," which means you pay the lawyer nothing if you don't receive a settlement. This is how my office handles car accident cases.

In addition to the retainer agreement, lawyers in Florida are required to provide a copy of the Statement of Client's Rights. It's a two-page document for all car accident/injury victims that is included in the first appendix in the back of this book for your convenience.

The lawyer's office will likely have you fill out some type of questionnaire that includes demographic information about you and your contact information. It may also ask you for details about the accident, past car accident cases, and relevant medical history that might affect your case.

If you have any pictures, then the lawyer's office should ask you for those at this time as well. The lawyer's office may also send someone to take pictures of your car or will send someone to the scene of the accident if there is important information there.

Step Two: Sending Letters of Representation

The next step is quick. It is a letter of representation to all parties involved in the accident. My office will typically send a letter to all insurance companies that includes

- a request to direct all further communication to my office;
- a request to find out how much insurance coverage is available and the types of insurance; and
- a request that the insurance companies confirm in writing their position on liability.

In Florida, the insurance companies are obligated to respond within thirty days with the limits of liability insurance. My office will mail, fax, and even e-mail the letters of representation to the insurance companies so that they can get this information more quickly.

Step Three: Confirming the Insurance Coverage over the Phone

Immediately after the letters of representation get sent out, my office is on the phone with the insurance companies to find out if there is insurance coverage available. I can't tell you how many times people forget to pay their insurance bill or purposely don't have insurance. I've seen people buy insurance an hour after they were in a car accident. I've seen people who bought fake insurance cards, thinking they were being smart. Countless others buy "off-brand" auto insurance, only to find out that no one answers the phone when they want to file a claim. There is an insurance company in Miami that sells thousands of insurance policies a year and only has five employees. Do you think they answer the phone when you call?

It's important to understand the types of coverage available, which are as follows:

PIP no-fault coverage: This coverage will provide up to $10,000 per person injured in a car accident. Everyone involved in the accident goes through their own auto insurance for these benefits even if they are at fault for the accident. If you own a car in Florida, then you go through your auto insurance. If you don't own a car in Florida, then you go through the auto insurance of a resident relative (assuming you live with a relative who has auto insurance). As a failsafe, if you don't own a car in Florida and you don't live with a relative, then you go through the auto insurance of the vehicle that you were in at the time of the car accident. This way, 99 percent of people injured in a car accident can obtain medical treatment for their injuries, regardless of fault. There is nothing worse than being injured *and* having unpaid medical bills that put you in debt.

Bodily injury (BI) coverage: This coverage is purchased by the at-fault driver and pays out money to the parties who are injured from a car accident. BI coverage can be in many different amounts, from $10,000 (the minimum in Florida) to $1 million or more. Just because you are injured in a car accident due to someone else's negligence doesn't mean that you receive a check for the full amount of coverage. You still have to prove that you suffered a permanent injury and/or have unpaid medical bills, lost wages, pain and suffering, and so forth. This is what you hire a lawyer for.

Uninsured/underinsured motorist (UM) coverage: This coverage is purchased for your own benefit and the benefit of people injured while inside your car. Let's say the at-fault driver didn't have BI coverage for some reason or that the at-fault driver only had a small amount of BI coverage. If this is the case, then you can utilize your UM coverage.

Property damage coverage: This coverage only repairs cars that are damaged by the at-fault driver. It doesn't pay for damage to your car if you caused the accident.

Collision coverage: This coverage will cover the repairs to your vehicle even if you caused the accident.

Example:
Scott was driving his 1999 Toyota Camry and rearended Khloe. His girlfriend Kourtney was a passanger in his car. He was drinking and driving. Scott doesn't have any assets besides his car, and it's not likely that Scott will ever have any assets. Scott did have $10,000 per person/$20,000 per accident in BI coverage, which is the minimum required in Florida. Kourtney did not have UM coverage, but Khloe had UM coverage of $100,000. The maximum that Kourtney would recover for her injuries from this accident is the $10,000 BI.

The maximum that Khloe could recover for her injuries is the $10,000 BI coverage from Scott's insurance plus $100,000 from her UM coverage. Scott was at fault for the accident, so he can't recover any money for his injuries, but he can use his PIP no-fault insurance.

Example:
Mark caused an accident with Julius. Mark's property damage coverage will pay to repair Julius's car. Mark was smart enough to buy collision coverage, so his insurance company is paying to repair his car too.

Step Four: Requesting Medical Records and Obtaining Documentation to Attach to the Demand Letter

Once you have concluded treatment with all of your doctors and have a good grip on what still hurts from the car accident, it is time for your lawyer to start requesting your medical records.

This process usually starts around four to six months after the date of the car accident, but every case is a little different. I try to meet with every client in person a couple of times by this point, and we would also have had several phone calls. Injured clients should have already had their MRI scans by this point and may have undergone an injection or two by now.

This request might seem easy—just tell the doctors to send you your medical records. This is actually one of the most time- and energy-consuming steps. I've burned a lot of bridges with doctors who have lost medical records. I've refused to let my clients see some doctors because they have burned me so badly in the past with medical records. I had a doctor in Saint Lucie, for example, who took six months to photocopy patients' medical charts. I got fed up and had to send an employee to her office with a scanner so that we could scan the files in the doctor's office. The doctor's office could only produce three out of the four patient files. Following the visit, it still took a lot of text messages and phone calls to the doctor to get the clients' medical bills as well.

Another doctor told me that his computer crashed and that he couldn't produce records for his patient/my client. This meant that I had to submit my client's demand letter package with the statement, "My client's doctor couldn't produce four months of medical records reflecting my client's pain and treatment." This seriously impacted the settlement of the case. I avoid these doctors like the plague, but for every doctor like this whom I refuse to work with, another one pops up in his or her place.

I had another doctor who produced handwritten bills for five months' worth of treatment. That was the first and only time I've ever seen handwritten bills. Those pretty much went extinct when they invented easy-to-use billing software about twenty years ago. It costs about $100 for the software! I won't work with that doctor either.

Getting hospital records is another story. All hospitals are paperless, so getting the medical file should be quick and easy, right? Wrong! They take months to respond and then send us a bill for $100+ for the medical records even though there are state and federal laws regulating how much they can charge for medical records—let alone the fact that the client would be dead if the information in those medical records was needed for a life-or-death emergency.

Some other documents that we request for our file include the bills to repair the client's vehicle and photos of all vehicles involved in the accident. We might already have this information, but sometimes there are supplemental repair bills, so we double-check.

We also request things like gym logs if the accident resulted in a change in the client's fitness routine. For example, I represented one client who hit the gym every day for a year straight. After the accident, my client stopped going to the gym for three months because of the pain. After that, my client went back to the gym but sporadically. We used that gym log from LA Fitness to increase the compensation to our client. It showed two things: (1) our client was injured, and (2) our client had paperwork showing her loss of enjoyment.

I represented a couple who had to cancel a cruise because they were injured very badly on the way to the port and missed the departure because they were at the hospital. The money that they lost on the trip was reimbursable. It wasn't a ten-year anniversary cruise or anything monumental, so they didn't really receive much compensation in the way of loss of enjoyment because they could still book another cruise, but they were happy with recovering the money so that they could book another cruise.

Another couple I represented had been together for ten years and spent time doing all sorts of crazy things—like horseback riding, cave spelunking, and sailing from the USA to Central America on their boat. They couldn't do these things after the car accident, so we included photos that showed them enjoying these activities. We got them a sizeable settlement because of it.

By this time, we usually have the police report, but it is worth mentioning that we always attach the police report to our demand. I've seen some pretty good police reports, including one where my client was rear-ended by someone who fled the scene of the accident. My client followed in hot pursuit and called the police while she was chasing the hit-and-run driver. The police showed up and talked with the hit-and-run driver, who smelled strongly of alcohol. Turns out she had pills all over the floor and a bottle of vodka too. We underlined the juicy parts in the narrative section of the police report and bolded them in our demand letter. This case settled for three times as much as usual because of the narrative in the police report. It showed what a scumbag the at-fault driver was: (1) drunk, (2) popping pills, and (3) fleeing the scene of the accident. These facts were so damning that the insurance adjuster was begging to settle this case and more than doubled his initial offer, which was high to begin with.

Sometimes we will include lost wages when applicable. This is easy when the client can get a letter from the human resources department that states how much money the client makes per hour and how many hours/shifts the client missed from the accident. This is rarely the case. Most employers shy away from writing these kinds of letters because they don't want to get involved or think they will be dragged into a lawsuit. I have some clients who work at restaurants and receive mostly cash in the form of tips, so they can't properly document their lost wages with paystubs.

My clients who are self-employed oftentimes claim that they lost thousands of dollars, but this is difficult to prove when looking at their tax returns. Some of these clients either have a lot of tax write-offs that probably aren't 100 percent kosher, so they don't want to provide their tax returns, or they have large fluctuations from year to year. which makes it really difficult to prove lost wages.

The bottom line is that providing documentation of lost wages is usually very difficult, but we like to include this information when possible.

My office also includes a mileage count and asks for reimbursement for that as well. We calculate the distance from the client's home to the doctor's office using MapQuest.

One time early in my career, I made the mistake of including a background check on an at-fault driver showing that the individual had a lot of assets and owned a lot of corporations. It got included by mistake because it was attached to another document. When the adjuster saw this, she got so uptight and claimed that I was inflating the value of the case because the at-fault driver was wealthy. The adjuster claimed I was targeting the insured because he was wealthy. We eventually settled that case for the policy limits but for slightly different reasons. I bring this up because attaching too much information can be a problem too.

MRI reports are critical to include in a demand package. If the client has neck pain but never got a neck MRI scan, I will often send the client back to his or her doctor to get the MRI done. Insurance companies oftentimes exclude a neck injury from their evaluation if there is no MRI evidence. Remember, you need to prove your injuries, and MRI is the gold standard.

Any receipts for prescription drugs or other copays, deductibles, and so forth are typically requested by my office so that we can include these expenses in our demand letter.

When clients have scars from an accident or have scarring following surgery, we attach photos of that as well. Scars resulting from an accident increase the value of a claim.

Every case is unique, and we attach different documents as needed.

Step Five: Drafting a Demand Letter

M y office has a standard five-page demand letter that we use as an outline. We add/remove certain portions depending on the case, but there is no sense in starting from scratch for every case.

Most law firms, including ours, include the following information in the demand letter:

1. A liability section explaining why the at-fault party was negligent;

2. A medical treatment section explaining the most relevant parts of the medical treatment (e.g., which body parts had pain based on the records, which tests were ordered and the results, MRI results, other diagnostic test results, frequency of treatment, important medical findings, surgical recommendations, etc.)–basically, this section covers who the client saw, what the client complained of, what treatment the client received, and the what the doctors recommended;

3. A medical expenses section detailing all of the doctor's bills incurred and how much money was paid to those doctors;

4. A demand for the coverage limits or a lesser amount depending on the unique facts of the case (e.g., there is no point in asking for a million dollars on a case worth a few thousand); the demand is conditioned on the receipt of a fully completed financial affidavit that we attach, a reasonable release, a time requirement for the insurance company to issue the policy limits, and a written waiver of subrogation of any underinsured motorist coverage if applicable;

5. A request for an explanation of the insurance company's offer, which we include to make the adjuster think twice about giving our client a

low-ball offer; in addition, there is a Florida statute directly on point requiring the insurer to provide this information; and

6. Generic language indicating that the offer to settle can be changed or cancelled at any time.

The information in this list covers the standard elements of a demand letter; we will always add or subtract information depending on the client's unique case.

For example, I once sent a demand with more than five hundred pages of medical records, bills, and supporting documentation. The client had spent a few months in the hospital after being struck by a car as a pedestrian.

I've also sent a demand letter with the only document that I had, which was a death certificate. My client was a bicyclist who was struck by a car at full speed and died at the scene. There was a bicycle lane, and the assumption was that my client had been riding his bike in the middle of this lane when he was struck by the driver of a car who swerved into the bicycle lane. There were no witnesses besides the driver of the car, and she didn't remember seeing my client until after the impact. There was no police report at the time because it was still being investigated by the homicide detectives, and they take their time and gather all of the evidence before issuing a report. Everyone assumed that the driver of the car, a little old lady, had caused the accident by swerving into the bicycle lane and striking my client.

A few months after the case settled for the policy limits, the homicide detective reached out to me and forwarded me a copy of the final investigative report. It turns out that the detective had been waiting for several months for a toxicology report. It showed that my client's blood alcohol level was three times the legal limit to drive a car. Although we don't have any definitive proof, it seems likely that my client was at fault for the accident and probably swerved into the car lane because he was drunk. You are not entitled to money after a car accident if you are at fault.

Step Six: Responding to the Settlement Offer

After a demand letter and the attachments are received by the insurance company, it usually has thirty days to respond with an offer.

My demand letter includes a section asking the insurance adjuster to provide a written explanation of the factors that the insurance company considered when making an offer that is less than the policy limits. Sometimes insurance companies include this information, and other times they don't. Florida statutes require the adjuster to promptly provide a reasonable explanation in writing for the offer of a settlement. If we get a low-ball offer, then we will try to pin the adjuster down by getting the adjuster to provide an explanation for the dollar figure given in a response letter.

Sometimes the insurance companies will offer the policy limits based on the medical treatment received, the property damage, and the unique facts of the case.

More often, the insurance company offers less than the policy limits, and we have to negotiate a settlement. When the insurance company offers less than the policy limits, I will meet with the client to discuss a couple of things. First, I would want to know if the client still has a lot of pain from the accident. If the client still has a lot of pain, then I discuss the options with the client and let him or her know that once the case is settled, there is no going back. If the client needs to take painkillers for the rest of his or her life, for example, then it is coming out of the client's pocket after we settle the case. If the client needs to get surgery in three years because he or she is still in a lot of pain, then that is coming out of the client's pocket after we settle the case. Remember, insurance companies aren't handing out bags of money, and they aren't going to write you a check for getting surgery three years after an accident. They are the ultimate poker players, and they will tell you that they will be happy to pay for surgery if you get it now; otherwise, they won't pay.

If we get a low-ball offer to settle from the insurance company, I will fight for my clients to get a fair settlement offer. But at the same time, the client needs to fight too. If the client won't get an injection to reduce his or her pain (especially when the insurance company will pay for it), then the client is showing me (and possibly a jury if we file a lawsuit) that he or she isn't *seriously* injured.

I understand that some of my clients are scared of getting an injection. The injections can be performed under local or general anesthesia. You can literally be "put to sleep" for ten minutes to get an injection if you are that scared. If that injection reduces pain from a level nine down to a level three, then why wouldn't a person injured in a car accident get the injection, especially when the insurance company will pay the bill for it?

I had a client who was seriously injured after an accident, and when we got a $6,000 offer, I knew I had to meet with the client in person because he would be extremely upset to know that the insurance company didn't care about the pain that he had from the car accident. After a thirty-minute meeting, the client decided that he needed to go back to his pain management doctor and schedule the epidural steroid injection that the doctor had previously recommended. The client called me a few days after the injection to tell me that he wished he had gotten the injection months ago and didn't care about getting any money from the settlement. I eventually settled the case for about $50,000, but knowing that my client didn't have bad pain anymore was more rewarding.

I had another client who had extreme weakness in his knee after bumping it in the car accident. He was very scared of the surgery, but I had him meet with another client who had undergone the same knee surgery just three days earlier. The two talked about the surgery one-on-one, and he decided to get the knee surgery after realizing the benefits. Knee surgery is expensive if you have to pay out of pocket for it. Why not have the auto insurance pay for the knee surgery and pay for the days you miss from work while you recuperate? Why should the insurance company get a break when you didn't?

Step Seven: Negotiating or Filing Suit

At the end of the day, your lawyer will decide whether it is best to negotiate your case and settle it without having to go to court or if filing a lawsuit is in your best interest.

Sometimes lawyers can take an entire year to negotiate a case if they think the insurance company is being reasonable. Sometimes I file suit the same day we receive an offer to settle if the insurance adjuster makes a ridiculous/insulting offer.

For example, I had an insurance adjuster call me to tell me that he would "never pay on this bullshit claim." I immediately filed the lawsuit. My client was T-boned by his insured, and they treated my client like she was at fault for the accident. After I was able to depose everyone involved in the accident, I found out that the other driver who T-boned my client had been arrested multiple times in a couple of different states for violence and drug offenses. He also admitted to drinking and smoking weed an hour prior to the accident. He also admitted that he was at fault for the accident. You can imagine that the insurance company eventually paid me a lot of money to settle that case after we took all the depositions.

Sometimes I file a lawsuit because I know that the adjuster is a complete moron and I want the insurance company to hire an attorney to look at the file. On that same note, I don't file a lawsuit in some cases because I know which attorney will get the case. Some of the lawyers that represent insurance companies "drink the Kool-Aid," meaning that they are so narrow-minded and one-sided that they think every car accident case is fraudulent or exaggerated. In those cases I might wait a little while to decide because adjusters will move around or get a different position. Sometimes a new adjuster will get assigned the file, and that new adjuster might evaluate the case differently.

Don't be fooled, though. I know that not every case is worth spending six months negotiating or filing a lawsuit over. If there is very little property damage, and my client has been in three car accidents in the last two years, I'm not always going to rush to the courthouse to file a lawsuit.

Clients need to understand that lawsuits take a long time. The courts are government-run agencies, so they are slow to begin with. Add to that the fact that the insurance company lawyers are experts in dragging the case out even longer. They always ask for extensions and delay the scheduling of hearings and depositions. They purposely don't respond to e-mails, phone calls, and paperwork. I've probably filed hundreds of Motions for Sanctions against of Motions for Sanctions against insurance companies for their delay tactics.

I once filed a Motion to Show Cause for Failing to Comply with a Prior Court Order Compelling Discovery and attached Ex Parte Orders Requesting Sanctions and a Writ of Bodily Attachment against a lawyer who took over a year to provide me with a copy of the claims file in a lawsuit against Progressive—in plain English, basically, I asked the judge to issue a warrant for the arrest of the attorney on the file for failing to provide information related to the accident after the court had ordered him to do so. The judge never signed the order issuing the writ/warrant, but the lawyer was so freaked out that he sent me the entire claim file overnight by FedEx. I had such a solid paper trail in that case that the lawyer knew he pushed the limits of failing to respond. That lawyer kept telling me the case was fraudulent and that he had so much evidence against my client, but he obviously didn't—otherwise, the insurance company wouldn't have paid my client a lot of money to settle the lawsuit.

Appendix
Statement of Client's Rights

Before you, the prospective client, arrange a contingency fee agreement with a lawyer, you should understand this statement of your rights as a client. This statement is not a part of the actual contract between you and your lawyer, but, as a prospective client, you should be aware of these rights.

1. There is no legal requirement that a lawyer charge a client a set fee or a percentage of money recovered in a case. You, the client, have the right to talk with your lawyer about the proposed fee and to bargain about the rate or percentage as in any other contract. If you do not reach an agreement with one lawyer, you may talk with other lawyers.

2. Any contingency fee contract must be in writing, and you have three business days to reconsider the contract. You may cancel the contract without any reason if you notify your lawyer in writing within three business days of signing the contract. If you withdraw from the contract within the first three days, you do not owe the lawyer a fee, although you may be responsible for the lawyer's actual costs during that time. But if your lawyer begins to represent you, your lawyer may not withdraw from the case without giving you notice, delivering the necessary papers to you, and allowing you time to employ another lawyer. Often, your lawyer must obtain court approval before withdrawing from a case. If you discharge your lawyer without good cause after the three-day period, you may have to pay a fee for the work the lawyer has done.

3. Before hiring a lawyer, you, the client, have the right to know about the lawyer's education, training, and experience. If you ask, the lawyer should tell you specifically about the lawyer's actual experience dealing with cases similar to yours. If you ask, the lawyer should provide information about specific training or knowledge and give you this information in writing if you request it.

4. Before signing a contingency fee contract with you, a lawyer must advise you whether the lawyer intends to handle your case alone or whether other lawyers will be helping with the case. If your lawyer intends to refer the case to other lawyers, the lawyer should tell you what kind of fee-sharing arrangement will be made with the other lawyers. If lawyers from different law firms will represent you, at least one lawyer from each law firm must sign the contingency fee contract.

5. If your lawyer intends to refer your case to another lawyer or counsel with other lawyers, your lawyer should tell you about that at the beginning. If your lawyer takes the case and later decides to refer it to another lawyer or to associate with other lawyers, you should sign a new contract that includes the new lawyers. You, the client, also have the right to consult with each lawyer working on your case, and each lawyer is legally responsible for representing your interest and is legally responsible for the acts of other lawyers involved in the case.

6. You, the client, have the right to know in advance how you will need to pay the expenses and the legal fees at the end of the case. If you pay a deposit in advance for costs, you may ask reasonable questions about how the money will be or has been spent and how much of it remains unspent. Your lawyer should give a reasonable estimate about future necessary costs. If your lawyer agrees to lend or advance you money to prepare or research the case, you have the right to know periodically how much money your lawyer has spent on your behalf. You also have the right to decide, after consulting with your lawyer, how much money is to be spent to prepare a case. If you pay the expenses, you have the right to decide how much to spend. Your lawyer should also inform you whether the fee will be based on the gross amount recovered or the amount recovered minus the costs.

7. You, the client, have the right to be told by your lawyer about possible adverse consequences if you lose the case. Those adverse consequences might include money that you might have to pay to your lawyer for costs and the liability you might have for attorney's fees for the other party.

8. You, the client, have the right to receive and approve a closing statement at the end of the case before you pay any money. The statement must list all of the financial details of the entire case, including the amount recovered, all expenses, and a precise statement of your lawyer's fee. Until you approve the closing statement, you need not pay any money to anyone, including your lawyer. You also have the right to have every lawyer or law firm working on your case sign this closing statement.

9. You, the client, have the right to ask your lawyer at reasonable intervals how the case is progressing and to have these questions answered to the best of your lawyer's ability.

10. You, the client, have the right to make the final decision regarding settlement of a case. Your lawyer must notify you of all offers of settlement before and after the trial. Offers during the trial must be immediately communicated, and you should consult with your lawyer regarding whether to accept a settlement. However, you must make the final decision to accept or reject a settlement.

11. If at any time, you, the client, believe that your lawyer has charged an excessive or illegal fee, you have the right to report the matter to the Florida Bar, the agency that oversees the practice and behavior of all lawyers in Florida. For information on how to reach the Florida Bar, call (800)342-8060, or contact the local bar association. Any disagreement between you and your lawyer about a fee can be taken to court, and you may wish to hire another lawyer to help you resolve this disagreement. Usually fee disputes must be handled in a separate lawsuit, unless your fee contract provides for arbitration. You can request, but you may not require, that a provision for arbitration (under Chapter 682 of the Florida Statutes or under the fee arbitration rule of the Rules Regulating the Florida Bar) be included in your fee contract.

_____

CLIENT SIGNATURE

Initial Settlement Offers
and Final Amounts

This section will show you just how much insurance companies like to negotiate.

This section will show you exactly why you need a lawyer. On the left-hand side, you will see the insurance company's initial offer. On the right-hand side, you will see what the insurance company paid out.

This is why you need a lawyer. We negotiate with the insurance companies daily and know how much your case is worth.

For the privacy of our clients, we have deleted certain information.

USAA   4/7/2015 11:51:39 AM PAGE   2/002 Fax Server

9800 Fredericksburg Road
San Antonio, TX 78288

USAA®

ABRAHAM S OVADIA, ESQ.   April 7, 2015
FLORIDA PIP LAW FIRM, P.A.
4800 NORTH FEDERAL HWY, SUITE
BOCA RATON FL 33431-5188

Reference: ████████

Dear Abraham S Ovadia, Esq.,

I am writing regarding the claim referenced below.

Policyholder:
Reference #:   ████████
Date of loss: August 29, 2014
Location of loss: Boca Raton, Florida

In response to the BI demand that we have reviewed for ████████, we are offering $15,000 to settle this claim. Please relay this offer to your client and contact me at your convenience.

You may submit correspondence or questions to me. My contact information is:

Address: Auto Injury Solutions
                Attn: USAA Medical Mail Dept.
                P.O. Box 26001
                Daphne, AL 36526
Fax: ████████
Phone: ████████

Sincerely,

████████

USAA Southeast Regional Office
United Services Automobile Association
████████

EF/EQS

cc : ████████

000537452 - DM-04664 - 560 - 7941 - 31   54577-0914

                                                                Page 1 of 1

46

MAIL DIRECT

03292.1XZ2D.JS$1062420902.01.01.11916
FLORIDA PIP LAW FIRM TRUST ACCOUNT
4800 N FEDERAL HWY
STE D204
BOCA RATON, FL 334315188

United Services Automobile Association
PO Box 33490
San Antonio, TX 78265

INVOICE #:
USAA #:
LOSS RPT #: 560
LOSS DATE: 08/29/2014
POLICYHOLDER:

LOB: AUT
CLAIMS REP:
CHECK #: 0011621877
CHECK DATE: 06/09/2015

EXPLANATION OF PAYMENT	TOTAL PAYMENT AMOUNT
Payment under Bodily Injury Liability coverage FOR THE BENEFIT OF	$**75,000.00

0011621877

United Services Automobile Association
PO Box 33490
San Antonio, TX 78265

51-44/119 CT

DATE
06/09/2015

CHECK AMOUNT
$**75,000.00

PAY **Seventy-Five Thousand and 00/100 s**

TO THE ORDER OF: FLORIDA PIP LAW FIRM TRUST ACCOUNT

USAA #:   / LR #: 560

NATURE OF PAYMENT:
Payment under Bodily Injury Liability coverage FOR THE BENEFIT OF

BANK OF AMERICA - HARTFORD, CT   VOID 180 DAYS FROM ISSUE DATE   AUTHORIZED SIGNATURE

⑇0011621877⑇ ⑆011900445⑆ 2240015665⑈

GEICO.
gelco.com

GEICO General Insurance Company

Attn: Florida Claims, P.O. Box 9091
Macon, GA 31294-9248

04/17/2015

Florida Pip Law Firm, P.a
To Whom It May Concern
4800 N Federal Hwy STE 204D
Boca Raton, FL 33431-3413

Company Name: Geico General Insurance Company
Claim Number: ▓
Loss Date: Monday, December 8, 2014
Policyholder: ▓

To Whom It May Concern,

This will acknowledge receipt of your letter dated April 8,2015, demanding $100,000 to settle your client's claim. We called on April 16,2015 and we left a message for attorney . This will confirm that our insured's Bodily Injury liability limits are $100,000/$300,000.

We have reviewed the medical records for your client., ▓ We understand that your client treated after the accident with for a cut over her eye brow, which it appear she had to have stiches for. When your client presented herself urgent care she never mention any injuries to her neck or her back on the date of loss. It appears she waited almost a week post loss to follow up with a chiropractor for injuries alleged to her neck and back. Ms. ▓ treated with a chiropractor and orthopedic doctor for soft tissue injuries. Your client was diagnosed with herniation's and bulges in the cervical and lumbar spine. It's questionable if there was a threshold breached. We are requesting the MRI films for cervical and lumbar spine. We would like updated photos of the cut above her right eye also.

We are extending an offer of $10,000. Given the known facts of this loss and the medical documentation within our possession, we believe that we have made a fair and reasonable offer. You and your client should be advised that if additional information comes to light we have the right to adjust or withdraw our settlement offer at any time.

We look forward to hearing from your office so that we may continue to work to resolve this claim in a manner that is fair and equitable to all parties involved.

EC0020 (1/2007)

48

Detailed Payment Summary

GEICO GENERAL INSURANCE CO
Field Claim Center: 08 Florida

NO. N 176027291

Date: 09/10/2015

ONE GEICO CENTER
MACON, GA 31296-0001

Claim #:
Date of Loss: 12/08/2014

Claimant Name:
Insured Name:
Tax ID / SS# /   XX-XX
Atty ADJ Code:
Adjuster Code:

Pay To:
Florida PIP Law Firm PA Trust Account
A/B/O   , A Single Individual

Florida Pip Law Firm Pa
4800 N Federal Hwy Ste 204D
Boca Raton Fl 33431-3413

Total Amount:
$**100,000.00

Payment Type:
LOSS

IP AND FEATURE AND AMOUNT
02   RBI $*100000.00

In Payment Of
Bodily Injury Coverage
Bodily Injury Settlement

Visit geico.com

Now, parties involved in a GEICO claim can track the progress of the claim, view damage photos and more at geico.com! *GEICO policyholders can make a payment, change drivers or vehicles and request additional coverages.* Not insured with GEICO? 15 minutes could save you 15% or more on car insurance. Of course, we're also available for policy or claim service 24/7 at 1-800-841-3000.

* These online services are unavailable to Assigned Risk policyholders.

clmschok   PLEASE DETACH AND KEEP FOR YOUR RECORDS

GEICO GENERAL INSURANCE CO
ONE GEICO CENTER
MACON, GA 31296-0001

Bank of America
Hartford, CT 06120
Claim Number:

51-44
119 CT

NO. N 176027291

VOID AFTER 180 DAYS

Date: 09/10/2015

Claimant:

Insured Name:

Amount:
$**100,000.00

Feature Symbol & Amount
RBI $*100000.00

ONE-HUNDRED--THOUSAND*AND*00/100*DOLLARS

Pay to the Order of:
Florida PIP Law Firm PA Trust Account
A/B/O   , A Single Individual

In Payment of:
Bodily Injury Coverage
Bodily Injury Settlement

Mail To:
Florida Pip Law Firm Pa
4800 N Federal Hwy Ste 204D
Boca Raton Fl 33431-3413

⑈176027291⑈ ⑆011900445⑈ 000000019191⑈

GEICO.
geico.com

GEICO General Insurance Company

Attn: Florida Claims, P.O. Box 9091
Macon, GA 31294-9248

04/06/2015

Florida Pip Law Firm, P.a
To Whom It May Concern
4800 N Federal Hwy STE 204D
Boca Raton, FL 33431-3413

Company Name:	Geico General Insurance Company
Claim Number:	▮▮▮▮▮▮▮▮
Loss Date:	Monday, December 8, 2014
Policyholder:	▮▮▮▮▮▮

To Whom It May Concern,

This will acknowledge receipt of your letter dated April 3,2015, demanding $100,000 to settle your client's claim. We called on April 3,2015 and we left a message for ▮▮▮▮▮▮. This will confirm that our insured's Bodily Injury liability limits are $100,000/$300,000.

We have received your demand for ▮▮▮▮▮▮. We have reviewed the medical records for your client. We understand you client has treated with an orthopedic doctor as well as a chiropractor. Your client also treated with urgent care. It appears your client was diagnosed with a right shoulder tear and herniation in the cervical spine. We are requesting the MRI films for both the right shoulder and the cervical spine.

In order to continue the evaluation of the claim, we are extending an offer of $5,989.00. Given the known facts of this loss and the medical documentation within our possession, we believe that we have made a fair and reasonable offer. You and your client should be advised that if additional information comes to light we have the right to adjust or withdraw our settlement offer at any time.

We look forward to hearing from your office so that we may continue to work to resolve this claim in a manner that is fair and equitable to all parties involved.

Sincerely,

▮▮▮▮▮▮, Examiner Code ▮▮▮▮

EC0029 (1/2007)

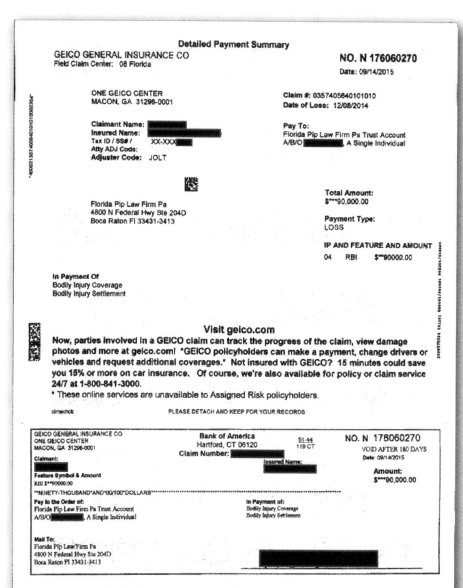

MetLife Auto & Home®
Tampa Field Claim Office
Attention: Claims
P.O. Box 30018
Tampa, FL 33630
(800) 854-6011

MetLife

July 1, 2015

Florida Pip Law Firm PA
4800 N Federal Hwy Suite D204
Boca Raton, FL 33431

Our Customer: ▓▓▓▓▓▓
Our Claim Number: ▓▓▓▓▓▓
Date of Loss: December 2, 2014
Your Client: ▓▓▓▓▓▓

Dear Mr Ovadia:

I am in receipt of your bodily injury demand for ▓▓▓▓▓▓ and thank you for same. Per the message left with your office, at this time we are extending an offer of $23,000 to resolve her claim.

Please contact me once you have discussed this offer with your client. Thank you.

We look forward to hearing from you soon.

Sincerely,

▓▓▓▓▓▓
Metropolitan Casualty Insurance Company
Senior Claim Adjuster
(800) 854-6011▓▓▓▓
Fax: (866)▓▓▓▓

FLORIDA LAW REQUIRES US TO NOTIFY YOU OF THE FOLLOWING: Any person who knowingly and with intent to injure, defraud, or deceive any insurance company files a statement of claim containing any false, incomplete, or misleading information is guilty of a felony of the third degree.

MetLife Auto & Home is a brand of Metropolitan Property and Casualty Insurance Company and its affiliates. Warwick, RI.

MPL OFFERAT

Printed in U.S.A 0698

52

0012
PO BOX 30018
TAMPA   FL 33630

MetLife Auto & Home

MetLife Auto & Home is a brand of
Metropolitan Property and Casualty Insurance Company
and its Affiliates, Warwick, RI

0012

TAD163630
FLORIDA PIP LAW FIRM PA
4800 N FEDERAL HWY STE 204D
BOCA RATON, FL 33431

INSURED:

CLAIMANT:

CHECK NUMBER :   008466243

CHECK AMOUNT: $70,000.00

Seventy Thousand and 0/100 Dollars

BODILY INJURY PAYMENT FOR CLAIMS ARISING FROM
LOSS OF 12-02-14

F1 DJ DJ 3104503   *

MetLife Auto & Home

PO BOX 30018
TAMPA   FL 33630
1-800-854-6011

METROPOLITAN CASUALTY INSURANCE COMPANY

0894

| BODILY INJURY PAYMENT FOR CLAIMS ARISING FROM LOSS OF 12-02-14 | | Check Number 008466243 |
| TIN | Claim No. | Not Valid Before 11-05-2015 |

Void Nine (9) Months
After This Date

Seventy Thousand and 0/100 Dollars

Pay to the Order of:

FLORIDA PIP LAW FIRM PA
4800 N FEDERAL HWY STE 204D
BOCA RATON, FL 33431

Citibank, N.A.
One Penn's Way
New Castle, DE 19720

Amount
*******$70,000.00

AUTHORIZED SIGNATURE

⑈008466243⑈ ⑆031100209⑆ 38755839⑈

Providing Insurance and Financial Services
Home Office, Bloomington, IL

State Farm®

May 29, 2015

Florida Pip Law Firm
4800 N Federal Hwy Ste 204d
Boca Raton FL 33431-3413

State Farm Claims
PO Box 106171
Atlanta GA 30348-6171

RE: Claim Number: ▮▮▮▮▮▮
      Date of Loss: December 13, 2014
      Our Insured: ▮▮▮▮▮▮
      Your Client: ▮▮▮▮▮▮

To Whom It May Concern:

We received your 05/18/2015 time limit demand for your client, ▮▮▮▮▮▮. We have concluded the evaluation of your client's claim resulting from this loss. Based on the documentation provided, State Farm® is willing to settle your client's claim for $15,500.

Please contact us once you have had an opportunity to review this offer.

Sincerely,

▮▮▮▮▮▮
Claim Specialist
(844) 292-8615 Ext. ▮▮▮▮▮▮
Fax: (855) 820-▮▮▮

State Farm Mutual Automobile Insurance Company

cc: ▮▮▮▮▮▮

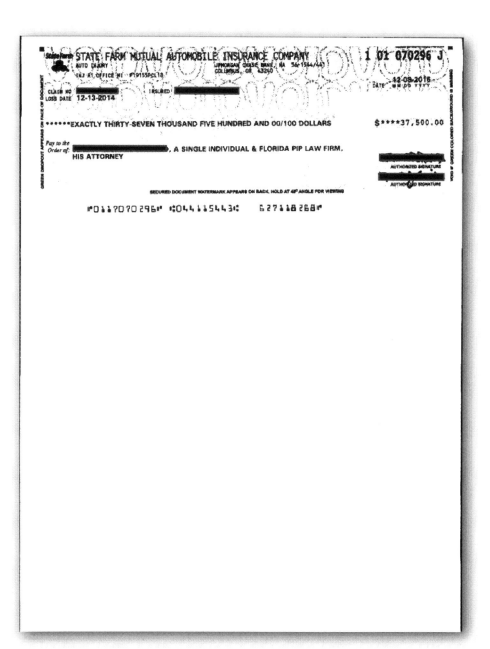

PROGRESSIVE CLAIMS
1641 WORTHINGTON ROAD
SUITE 200
WEST PALM BEACH, FL 33409

PROGRESSIVE™

Underwritten By:
Progressive American Insurance Company

Claim Number: ▮▮▮▮▮
Loss Date: March 27, 2015
Document Date: September 18, 2015
Page 1 of 1

FLORIDA PIP LAW FIRM
ABRAHAM OVADIA
4800 N FEDERAL HIGHWAY
STE D204
BOCA RATON, FL 33431

claims.progressive.com
Track the status and details of your claim,
e-mail your representative or report a
new claim.

Claim Information

Sent via mail and fax:

RE:Your Client : ▮▮▮▮▮

In response to your demand letter dated September 8, 2015 for your client, ▮▮▮▮▮ I am extending a settlement offer of $1,710.00 as full and final for his pending claim. Please discuss our settlement offer with your client and advise me of his decision.

Should you have any questions, please feel free to contact me at the number below.

▮▮▮▮▮
Claims Department
1-561-469-▮▮▮▮
1-800-PROGRESSIVE (1-800-776-4737)
Fax: 1-561-683-▮▮▮

cc: ▮▮▮▮▮

Form 2587 XX (01/08) - FL

Car Accident Claims: What You Need To Know!

PHILADELPHIA
INSURANCE COMPANIES
A Member of the Tokio Marine Group

Claims Department
P.O. Box 950, Bala Cynwyd, Pennsylvania 19004-0950
800.765.9749 • Fax: 800.685.9238 • PHLY.com

Sr. Claims Examiner
Direct Dial: 610-538-2660
@phly.com

July 22, 2015

Emailed: ▓@floridapiplawfirm.com
▓, Esquire
Florida PIP Law Firm. P.A.
4800 N. Federal Highway. D204
Boca Raton, FL 33431

Re: Your Client: ▓
     Date of Accident: 1/31/15
     Claim No.: ▓

Dear ▓:

This is in response to your June 4, 2015 policy limit time demand that was not received until July 17, 2015. As you are aware, this is a driver v. driver situation. The police were unable to determine who was at fault for this accident and our insured was in the middle of the intersection at the time of impact. Therefore, we have determined that this is a 50/50 liability.

With that being said, I have reviewed your demand package and I have Thirty-One Thousand Seven hundred Sixty-One Dollars ($31,761.00) to settle this matter. After you have spoken with your client, please contact me to discuss this matter.

I look forward to discussing this matter
Sincerely,

▓

Sr. Claims Examiner

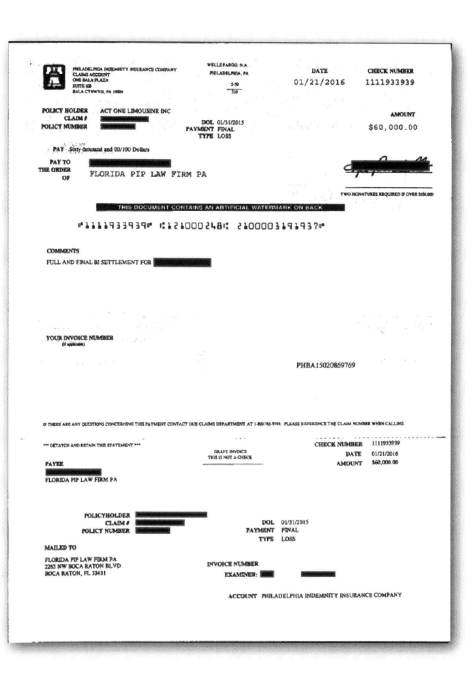

Abraham S. Ovadia

Providing Insurance and Financial Services
Home Office, Bloomington, IL

 StateFarm

September 25, 2015

Florida Pip Law Firm Pa
4800 N Federal Hwy Ste 204d
Boca Raton FL 33431-3413

State Farm Claims
PO Box 106171
Atlanta GA 30348-6171

RE: Claim Number:
      Date of Loss: February 23, 2015
      Our Insured:
      Policy Number:
      Your Client(s):

To Whom It May Concern:

State Farm Insurance is in receipt of your demand letter dated 9/23/2015, in order to properly evaluate your clients demand we are requesting additional information be provided:

Please provide the PIP payout sheet, and final report with impairment rating. As you are aware, this information is necessary so that State Farm can evaluate your client's current claim properly.

Based on the information presented to date we would like to extend an initial offer of $2,900.00 in order to settle your client's claim. Should you wish to provide the additional information requested for our review we would gladly accept and re-evaluate your client's claim at that time.

This offer is inclusive of all damages, known and unknown, and any liens, assignments or statutory rights of recovery.

Should you have any questions or need assistance with this request, please contact the undersigned at the number below.

Sincerely,

Claim Specialist
(844) 292-8615 Ext.
Fax: (855)

State Farm Mutual Automobile Insurance Company

cc:

60

PAYMENT NO 1 19 141433 J
PAYMENT AMOUNT $15,000.00
ISSUE DATE 01-26-2016
AUTHORIZED BY
PHONE (844) 292-

CLAIM NO
LOSS DATE 02-23-2015
POLICY NO
INSURED

FLORIDA PIP LAW FIRM PA
4800 N FEDERAL HWY STE 204D
BOCA RATON FL 33431-3413

START DATE 01-26-2016

REMARKS full and final settlement

COVERAGE DESCRIPTION
BODILY INJURY LIABILITY

ON BEHALF OF

AMOUNT
15,000.00

RETAIN STUB FOR RECORDS

STATE FARM MUTUAL AUTOMOBILE INSURANCE COMPANY
AUTO INJURY
TAX AT OFFICE 34 P1975SPCL18

JPMORGAN CHASE BANK, NA 56-4544/441
COLUMBUS, OH 43240

1 19 141433 J

01-26-2016
DATE MM DD YY YY

CLAIM NO
LOSS DATE 02-23-2015

INSURED

**********EXACTLY FIFTEEN THOUSAND AND 00/100 DOLLARS**

$****15,000.00

Pay to the
Order of: , INDIVIDUALLY AND AS HUSBAND AND WIFE
& FLORIDA PIP LAW FIRM PA, THEIR ATTORNEY

AUTHORIZED SIGNATURE

AUTHORIZED SIGNATURE

SECURED DOCUMENT WATERMARK APPEARS ON BACK, HOLD AT 45° ANGLE FOR VIEWING

⑈1917141433⑈ ⑇0441154430 ⑇⑇⑇1450870

Providing Insurance and Financial Services
Home Office, Bloomington, IL

State Farm

November 24, 2015

Florida Pip Law Firm Pa
4800 N Federal Hwy Ste 204d
Boca Raton FL 33431-3413

State Farm Claims
PO Box 106171
Atlanta GA 30348-6171

RE: Claim Number: ▮▮▮▮▮▮
      Date of Loss: March 31, 2015
      Our Insured: ▮▮▮▮▮▮
      Your Client: ▮▮▮▮▮▮

To Whom It May Concern:

We received your November 12, 2015 time limit demand for your client, ▮▮▮▮▮▮ We
have concluded the evaluation of your client's claim resulting from this loss. Based on the
documentation provided, State Farm® is willing to settle your client's claim for $13,000.00.

Please contact us once you have had an opportunity to review this offer.

Sincerely,

▮▮▮▮▮▮
Claim Specialist
(844) 292-8615 Ext.▮▮▮
Fax: (855) ▮▮▮▮▮▮

State Farm Fire and Casualty Company

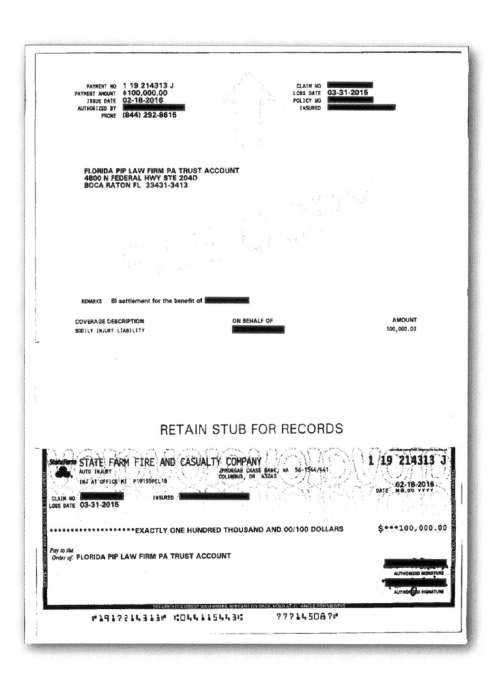

RETAIN STUB FOR RECORDS

Providing Insurance and Financial Services
Home Office, Bloomington, IL

State Farm

December 16, 2014

Abraham Ovadia, Esquire
Florida Pip Law Firm
4800 N Federal Hwy Ste 204d
Boca Raton FL 33431-3413

State Farm Claims
P.O. Box 106139
Atlanta GA 30348-6139

RE: Claim Number:
       Date of Loss: March 14, 2014
       Our Insured:
       Your Client:

Dear Mr. Ovadia:

This will confirm our settlement offer in the amount of $7,500 on December 16, 2014.

Please discuss this offer with your client and contact us at your convenience so we may bring this claim to a conclusion.

This settlement offer is inclusive of all damages, known and unknown, and any liens, assignments or statutory rights of recovery.

Thank you for your assistance.

Sincerely,

Claim Representative
(800) 879-   Ext.
Fax: (800) 627-4023

State Farm Mutual Automobile Insurance Company

cc:

Coral Springs, FL 33071-6111

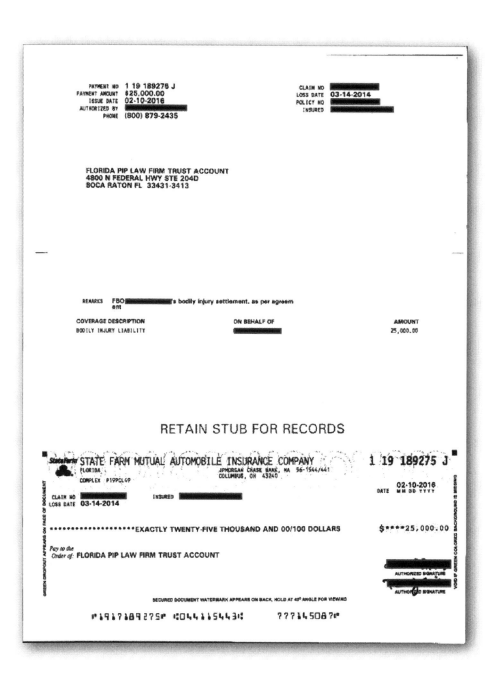

Abraham S. Ovadia

Providing Insurance and Financial Services
Home Office, Bloomington, IL.

StateFarm®

November 09, 2015

Florida Pip Law Firm, P.A.
4800 N Federal Hwy Ste 204d
Boca Raton FL 33431-3413

State Farm Claims
PO Box 106171
Atlanta GA 30348-6171

RE: Claim Number: █████████ Fax to 561-█████
  Date of Loss: April 23, 2015
  Our Insured: ██████████
  Your Client: ██████████

To Whom It May Concern:

This will confirm our settlement offer in the amount of $10,300.00 on November 9, 2015.

Please discuss this offer with your client and contact us at your convenience so we may bring this claim to a conclusion.

This settlement offer is inclusive of all damages, known and unknown, and any liens, assignments or statutory rights of recovery.

Thank you for your assistance.

Sincerely,

██████████
Claim Specialist
(844) 292-6615 Ext. ████████
Fax: (855) 820-████

State Farm Mutual Automobile Insurance Company

cc: ██████████

66

PAYMENT NO 1 19 291184 J
PAYMENT AMOUNT $25,900.00
ISSUE DATE 03-15-2016
AUTHORIZED BY
PHONE (844) 292-8615

CLAIM NO
LOSS DATE 04-23-2015
POLICY NO
INSURED

FLORIDA PIP LAW FIRM TRUST
4800 N FEDERAL HWY STE 204D
BOCA RATON FL 33431-3413

REMARKS //Full and final settlement for bodily injury

COVERAGE DESCRIPTION
BODILY INJURY LIABILITY

ON BEHALF OF

AMOUNT
25,900.00

RETAIN STUB FOR RECORDS

State Farm STATE FARM MUTUAL AUTOMOBILE INSURANCE COMPANY
AUTO INJURY
INJ A1 OFFICE DA PC00717.P078

JPMORGAN CHASE BANK, NA 56-1544/441
COLUMBUS, OH 43240

1 19 291184 J

DATE 03-15-2016
MM DD YYYY

CLAIM NO
LOSS DATE 04-23-2015

INSURED

*******EXACTLY TWENTY-FIVE THOUSAND NINE HUNDRED AND 00/100 DOLLARS

$****25,900.00

Pay to the
Order of: FLORIDA PIP LAW FIRM TRUST

AUTHORIZED SIGNATURE
AUTHORIZED SIGNATURE

SECURED DOCUMENT WATERMARK APPEARS ON BACK, HOLD AT 45° ANGLE FOR VIEWING

⑆1917291184⑆ ⑆044115443⑆ 777145087⑈

Progressive Claims Branch
1641 Worthington Rd #200
West Palm Beach, FL 33409
Ph # 561-402-██
Fax # 561-683-██

PROGRESSIVE

Underwritten by: Progressive American
Insurance Company
Claim number: ██
Date of loss: 8/18/14

Abraham Ovadia, Esq
4800 N Federal Highway D204
Boca Raton, FL 33431

Client: ██

Today's date: 3/25/15

Via fax and US Mail

Dear Mr Ovadia

This will serve as a response to your demand of March 11, 2015.

Please be advised that I have assumed the handling of this matter.

An offer of $14,000.00 is being conveyed to your client to resolve her pending injury claim.

Kindly convey the offer to your client and advise me thereafter of your position.

561-402-██

PROGRESSIVE

PAYABLE THROUGH
PNC BANK, N.A. 070
ASHLAND, OH
1-877-448-9544

VOID IF NOT PRESENTED WITHIN 90 DAYS

CLAIM NUMBER:
NAME:

DRAFT NUMBER:
2771839442

April 20, 2016

56-389

412

PAY EXACTLY $*********100,000.00

ONE HUNDRED THOUSAND AND 00/100 **

PAY TO
THE ORDER
OF:

FLORIDA PIP LAW FIRM PA TRUST ACCOUNT
4800 N FEDERAL HWY STE 204D
BOCA RATON, FL 33431-3413

Progressive American Insurance Company

BY:
AUTHORIZED SIGNATURE

⑈2771839442⑈ ⑆041203895⑇ 4239694516⑈

Providing Insurance and Financial Services
Home Office, Bloomington, IL

State Farm·

March 11, 2016

Abraham S Ovadia, Esquire
Florida PIP Law Firm, P.A.
4800 N Federal Hwy Ste 204d
Boca Raton FL 33431-3413

State Farm Claims
PO Box 106171
Atlanta GA 30348-6171

RE: Claim Number: ███████
       Date of Loss: August 26, 2015
       Our Insured:
       Your Client: ███████

Attorney Ovadia:

We received your February 23, 2016 time limit demand for your client, ███████. We have concluded the evaluation of your client's claim resulting from this loss. Based on the documentation provided, State Farm® is willing to settle your client's claim for $9,000.

This settlement is inclusive of all damages, known and unknown, and any liens, assignments or statutory rights of recovery.

Please contact us once you have had an opportunity to review this offer.

Sincerely,

███████

Claim Specialist
(972) ███████
Fax: (855) 820-███

State Farm Mutual Automobile Insurance Company

cc: ███████
     PO BOX ███
     FT LAUDERDALE, FL, 33307-0022

PAYMENT NO 1 19 408886 J
PAYMENT AMOUNT #100,000.00
ISSUE DATE 04-22-2016
AUTHORIZED BY
PHONE (844) 292-8615

CLAIM NO
LOSS DATE 08-26-2015
POLICY NO
INSURED

FLORIDA PIP LAW FIRM, P.A., TRUST ACCOUNT
4800 N FEDERAL HWY STE 204D
BOCA RATON FL 33431-3413

REMARKS **BODILY INJURY SETTLEMENT**

COVERAGE DESCRIPTION	ON BEHALF OF	AMOUNT
BODILY INJURY LIABILITY		100,000.00

RETAIN STUB FOR RECORDS

State Farm STATE FARM MUTUAL AUTOMOBILE INSURANCE COMPANY   1 19 408886 J
AUTO INJURY   JPMORGAN CHASE BANK, NA 56-1544/441
INJ A1 OFFICE 0A PC90717.P07B   COLUMBUS, OH 43240

04-22-2016
DATE MM DD YYYY

CLAIM NO
LOSS DATE 08-26-2015   INSURED

*********************EXACTLY ONE HUNDRED THOUSAND AND 00/100 DOLLARS $***100,000.00

Pay to the
Order of: FLORIDA PIP LAW FIRM, P.A., TRUST ACCOUNT

AUTHORIZED SIGNATURE

AUTHORIZED SIGNATURE

SECURED DOCUMENT WATERMARK APPEARS ON BACK, HOLD AT 45° ANGLE FOR VIEWING

⑈1917408886⑈ ⑆044115443⑈   ⑈⑈714508⑈⑈

South Florida Casualty
4443 LYONS RD., SUITE 201A
COCONUT CREEK FL 33073

FLORIDA PIP LAW FIRM PA
4800 N FEDERAL HWY STE 204D
BOCA RATON FL 334313413

June 03, 2016

INSURED:
DATE OF LOSS: October 16, 2015
CLAIM NUMBER:

PHONE NUMBER: 888-839-▮▮▮
FAX NUMBER: 877-619-▮▮▮
OFFICE HOURS: Mon - Fri 8:00 am - 5:30 pm,
Sat 8:00 am - 2:00 pm

YOUR CLIENT(S):

Dear Mr. Ovadia:

I am in receipt of your demand dated May 19th 2016 for the above mentioned client.

I have reviewed the information provided and I am extending an offer of $4000.00 to settle your client's bodily injury claim.

Based on my review of the records, it does appear to be a soft tissue injury claim. This was a minor impact with no injury at the scene, no emergency room treatment and initial delay of treatment of 3 days. Your client sought treatment with a chiropractor and treated for 6 months for a total of 49 visits which does appear excessive based on this minor impact. He also saw a specialist, Dr.▮▮▮ who recommended surgery yet there was no real radicular complaints and his records note neurological intact.

Kindly present my offer to your client and I look forward to your response.

Sincerely,

888-839-6150 Ext.▮▮▮
Allstate Fire and Casualty Insurance Company

Copy :

GEN1001   0388549347 GCC

INSURED:
CLAIMANT:
IN PAYMENT OF LOSS ON 10/16/2015.

POLICY NUMBER | CLAIM NUMBER
TAX ID.
DESK LOC | EMPLOYEE ID
GSB
Bank of America N.A. | Bank of America
Atlanta Deposit City Georgia | Customer Connection

64-1278
611

PAY: ONE HUNDRED THOUSAND DOLLARS AND ZERO CENTS

100,000.00

Allstate

INVOICE NUMBER | MCO | DATE ISSUED | 185510787
| 2470 | 08/03/2016

TO THE ORDER OF
_____ AND FLORIDA PIP LAW FIRM PA
4800 N FEDERAL HWY STE 204D
BOCA RATON FL 33431

COMPANY: ALLSTATE FIRE AND CASUALTY INSURANCE COMPANY

VOID IF NOT PRESENTED WITHIN THREE HUNDRED, SIXTY-FIVE DAYS OF DATE OF ISSUE

AUTHORIZED SIGNATURES

⑅185510787⑅ ⑈061112788⑈ 329 911 9562⑅

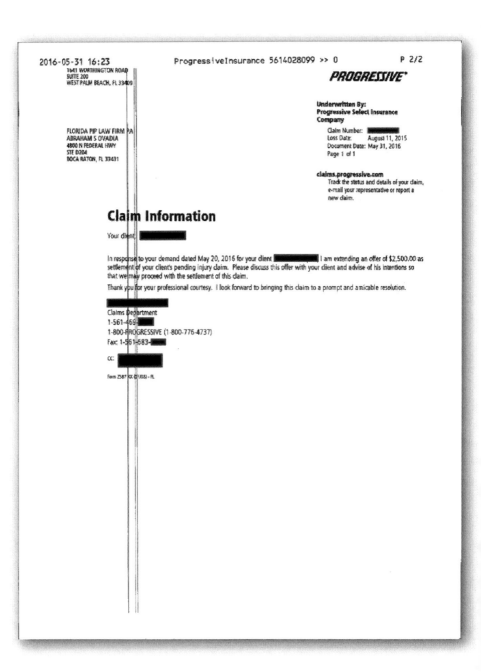

1641 WORTHINGTON ROAD
SUITE 200
WEST PALM BEACH, FL 33409

PROGRESSIVE®

Underwritten By:
Progressive Select Insurance Company

FLORIDA PIP LAW FIRM PA
ABRAHAM S OVADIA
4800 N FEDERAL HWY
STE D204
BOCA RATON, FL 33431

Claim Number: ▮▮▮▮▮▮▮
Loss Date: August 11, 2015
Document Date: May 31, 2016
Page 1 of 1

claims.progressive.com
Track the status and details of your claim, e-mail your representative or report a new claim.

Claim Information

Your client: ▮▮▮▮▮▮

In response to your demand dated May 20, 2016 for your client ▮▮▮▮▮▮▮▮ I am extending an offer of $2,500.00 as settlement of your client's pending injury claim. Please discuss this offer with your client and advise of his intentions so that we may proceed with the settlement of this claim.

Thank you for your professional courtesy. I look forward to bringing this claim to a prompt and amicable resolution.

▮▮▮▮▮▮▮▮

Claims Department
1-561-469-▮▮▮
1-800-PROGRESSIVE (1-800-776-4737)
Fax: 1-561-683-▮▮▮▮

cc: ▮▮▮▮▮▮

Form Z587 XX (1\08) - FL

PROGRESSIVE

PAYABLE THROUGH
PNC BANK, N.A. 070
ASHLAND,OH
1-877-448-9544

VOID IF NOT PRESENTED WITHIN 90 DAYS

CLAIM NUMBER: ▮▮▮▮▮
NAME: ▮▮▮▮▮▮▮

DRAFT NUMBER:
2772781185

56-389

412

September 23, 2016

PAY EXACTLY $*********100,000.00

ONE HUNDRED THOUSAND AND 00/100 ***

PAY TO
THE ORDER
OF

▮▮▮▮ AND FLORIDA PIP LAW FIRM PA
4800 N FEDERAL HWY STE 204D
BOCA RATON, FL 33431-3413

Progressive Select Insurance Company

BY ▮▮▮▮▮
AUTHORIZED SIGNATURE

⑆2772781185⑆ ⑈041203895⑈ 4239694516⑆

As per our conversation and in response to your demand for your client ▮▮▮▮▮▮▮▮, we are offering $15,000 to resolve this matter. At this time we must respectfully decline your demand. The offer is based on the merits of the claim as they have been presented. While we are making this offer to resolve, please consider the following merits:

- The bills were reduced significantly and the out pockets that remain are minimal.
- It is clearly evident that your client did not wear his seat belt in this loss contributing to his own injury.

In addition, please provide the final bills for further consideration and review:

- None of the bills have been reviewed through PIP and there is not a PIP log in your demand. If PIP was denied, please send a copy of the denial letter.

▮▮▮▮▮▮▮▮
Claim Service Analyst
Tampa Bay Casualty MCO - Major Represented

Allstate Insurance Company
740 Carillon Parkway Suite 400
St. Petersburg, FL 33716

Phone 727-571-▮▮▮
Fax 866-356-▮▮▮

Allstate Insurance Company - Claims Payment Processing
P.O. Box 660048 , Dallas, TX 75266 , United States

FLORIDA PIP LAW FIRM PA TRUST ACCOUNT F/
4800 N FEDERAL HWY STE 204D
BOCA RATON FL 33431-3413

Allstate.
You're in good hands.

11/07/2016

FLORIDA PIP LAW FIRM PA TRUST ACCOUNT F/,

ENCLOSED PLEASE FIND PAYMENT IN THE AMOUNT OF $52,500.00 FOR YOUR FULL AND FINAL SETTLEMENT OF ANY AND ALL CLAIMS FOR BODILY INJURY ARISING FROM LOSS OF 5/8/2015.

PLEASE REFERENCE CLAIM DETAILS BELOW.

CLAIM NUMBER:
DATE OF LOSS: 05/08/2015
INSURED:

In payment for Bodily Injury Liability for Date of Loss 5/8/2015.

ALLSTATE PROPERTY AND CASUALTY INSURANCE COMPANY
1-800-255-7828

0000020161107000285ZCT01001001000330

INSURED:
CLAIMANT:
IN PAYMENT OF, FULL AND FINAL SETTLEMENT OF ANY AND ALL CLAIMS
FOR BODILY INJURY ARISING FROM LOSS OF 5/8/2015.

PAY: FIFTY-TWO THOUSAND FIVE HUNDRED DOLLARS AND ZERO CENTS

POLICY NUMBER	CLAIM NUMBER
971034707	
TAX ID:	DESK LOC	EMPLOYEE ID
	DFA	84-1278
Bank of America, NA Atlanta,Dekalb Cnt,Georgia	Bank of America Customer Connection	611

52,500.00

Allstate

INVOICE NUMBER	MCO	DATE ISSUED	
	2470	11/07/2016	108321333

TO THE
ORDER
OF
FLORIDA PIP LAW FIRM PA TRUST ACCOUNT F/B/O
4800 N FEDERAL HWY STE D204
BOCA RATON FL 33431

COMPANY: ALLSTATE PROPERTY AND CASUALTY INSURANCE COMPANY

VOID IF NOT PRESENTED WITHIN THREE HUNDRED, SIXTY-FIVE DAYS OF DATE OF ISSUE

AUTHORIZED SIGNATURES

⑆108321333⑆ ⑈061112788⑈ 329 911 9562⑆

GEICO General Insurance Company

Attn: Florida Claims, P.O. Box 9091
Macon, GA 31208-9091

12/23/2015

Florida Pip Law Firm Pa
To Whom It May Concern
4800 N Federal Hwy STE 204D
Boca Raton, FL 33431-3413

Company Name: Geico General Insurance Company
Claim Number:
Loss Date: Monday, March 23, 2015
Policyholder:

To Whom It May Concern,

This will confirm receipt of your demand dated December 10, 2015 regarding your client,

As you know, we have paid $880.88 for the damages to your client's vehicle. Of that amount, only $207 was for parts. In review of the medicals presented, your client sought no hospital/emergency room treatment and his first initial evaluation was not until 15 days after the accident. He treated for soft tissue complaints and his diagnostic tests reveal 2 bulges with degeneration and no nerve or cord involvement.

In light of the extremely minor impact, it is difficult to relate the need for any treatment to this loss.

As such, we are making an offer of $500 and that is being made purely in the interest of settlement.

Upon receipt, kindly contact our office to further discuss settlement of this case.

Sincerely,

863-619-
Claims Department

EC0020 (1/2007)

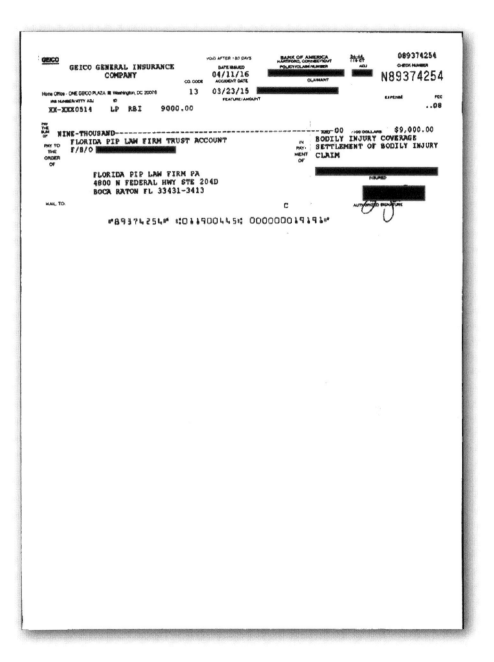

GEICO General Insurance Company

Attn: Florida Claims, P.O. Box 9091
Macon, GA 31208-9091

12/30/2015

Florida Pip Law Firm Pa
To Whom It May Concern
4800 N Federal Hwy STE 204D
Boca Raton, FL 33431-3413

Company Name: Geico General Insurance Company
Claim Number: █████████████
Loss Date: Thursday, April 2, 2015
Policyholder: ████████

To Whom It May Concern,

We are in receipt your bodily injury demand submitted on behalf of your client, ████████,
for the accident of April 2, 2015.

We have taken the time to review the specials you provided. It appears that your client
presented to ███████████████, one day after the accident, with complaints of low
back pain. ████████ indicated to the physician doctor that he had prior neck and back pain
from an accident in 2007. While your client's lumbar MRI indicated that there were bulges,
there were no acute findings. It appears the findings were pre-existing.

Based on all of the information available at this time, I am extending an offer of $2,000 to
resolve your client's bodily injury claim. Please present this offer, as well as the basis of our
offer, to your client.

Our objective continues to be the complete and equitable resolution of this claim at the
earliest date possible.

If you have any questions please contact me at the number listed below.

Sincerely,

████████
863-619-█████
Claims Department

EC0020 (1/2007)

Detailed Payment Summary

GEICO GENERAL INSURANCE CO
Field Claim Center: 08 Florida

NO. N 179997244

Date: 04/04/2016

ONE GEICO CENTER
MACON, GA 31296-0001

Claim #:
Date of Loss: 04/02/2015

Claimant Name:
Insured Name: Ms.
Tax ID / SS# / XX-XXX
Atty ADJ Code:
Adjuster Code:

Pay To:
Florida Pip Law Firm Pa
Trust Account f/b/o

Florida Pip Law Firm Pa
4800 N Federal Hwy Ste 204D
Boca Raton Fl 33431-3413

Total Amount:
$***50,000.00

Payment Type:
LOSS

IP AND FEATURE AND AMOUNT
02   RBI $***50000.00

In Payment Of
Bodily Injury Coverage
Bodily Injury Settlement

Visit geico.com

Now, parties involved in a GEICO claim can track the progress of the claim, view damage photos and more at geico.com! *GEICO policyholders can make a payment, change drivers or vehicles and request additional coverages.* Not insured with GEICO? 15 minutes could save you 15% or more on car insurance. Of course, we're also available for policy or claim service 24/7 at 1-800-841-3000.
* These online services are unavailable to Assigned Risk policyholders.

clmschck   PLEASE DETACH AND KEEP FOR YOUR RECORDS

GEICO GENERAL INSURANCE CO
ONE GEICO CENTER
MACON, GA 31296-0001

Bank of America
Hartford, CT 06120
Claim Number:

51-44
119 CT

NO. N 179997244
VOID AFTER 180 DAYS
Date: 04/04/2016

Claimant:

Insured Name:
Ms.

Amount:
$***50,000.00

Feature Symbol & Amount
RBI $**50000.00

FIFTY-THOUSAND*AND*00/100*DOLLARS*

Pay to the Order of:
Florida Pip Law Firm Pa
Trust Account f/b/o

In Payment of:
Bodily Injury Coverage
Bodily Injury Settlement

Mail To:
Florida Pip Law Firm Pa
4800 N Federal Hwy Ste 204D
Boca Raton Fl 33431-3413

⑈179997244⑈ ⑈011900445⑈ 000000019191⑈

Abraham S. Ovadia

GEICO.
geico.com

Government Employees Insurance Company

Attn: Florida Claims, P.O. Box 9091
Macon, GA 31208-9091

11/11/2015

Florida Pip Law Firm Pa
To Whom It May Concern
4800 N Federal Hwy STE 204D
Boca Raton, FL 33431-3413

Company Name: Government Employees Insurance Company
Claim Number: ███████
Loss Date: Wednesday, May 20, 2015
Policyholder: ███████
Driver: ███████
Your Client: ███████

To Whom It May Concern,

This letter is in response to the demand submitted by your client, ███████, dated October 27, 2015, to settle his Bodily Injury Claim for $50,000.00.

Based on the information he provided, it appears your client's injury was soft tissue in nature. He did not seek emergency medical care, but rather presented himself for passive treatment with the Chiropractor. The MRI your client underwent showed a herniated disc in the cervical spine along with a few bulges in his lumbar spine; however, no cord or nerve involvement was mentioned and no Needle EMG performed. Also this accident appears to be a low impact with a total of $1,283.57 being paid but less than $500 in parts. It is hard to understand how this low impact may of caused the bulges and herniations your client has.

Based on the information available to GEICO at this time, we are hereby offering $2,700.00 to settle your client's Bodily Injury Claim.

We ask that you relay this offer to your client, as well as our basis, and provide a response to GEICO as soon as one is known. Of course, we are always willing to review and consider any new information you may provide us and/or engage in settlement discussions.

Our objective continues to be the complete and equitable resolution of this claim at the earliest date possible.

EC0020 (1/2007)

82

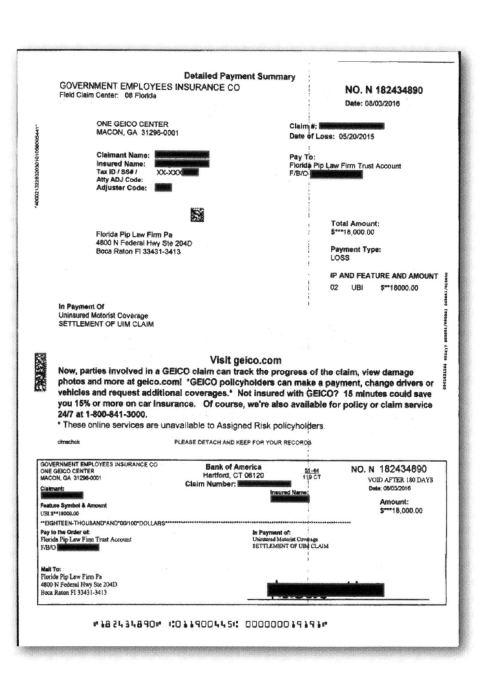

About the Ovadia Law Group

Ovadia Law Group was founded in February 2010. We initially started by only handling PIP suit claims for doctors but have expanded to several areas of practice.

Ovadia Law Group currently represents clients in the following areas of law:

- Car accident claims
- Slip-and-fall claims
- PIP suit claims for doctors

Ovadia Law Group prides itself on providing personal service to its clientele. Every client is assigned a case manager and also gets Abraham Ovadia's cell phone number: (561)305-6317. It's the same number Abraham Ovadia has had since high school.

About the Author

Abraham Ovadia, founder of Ovadia Law Group, graduated law school in May 2009 and passed his bar exam in September 2009. While attending law school, he worked for two years at a law firm in Miami that handled PIP suit claims for doctors. He learned a lot from that law firm, and after law school, he moved back to the Boca Raton area.

In February 2010, Abe officially opened his own law office out of the dining room of his mom's apartment. With $110,000 in student loan debt and no money to his name, Abraham worked all day and all night. Within a year, he had three employees and a small office space.

Within five years, Abraham had represented more than four hundred doctors' offices and collected millions of dollars against PIP insurers who wrongfully reduced doctors' bills. By the end of 2013, Abraham had filed more than five thousand lawsuits in more than thirty different counties in Florida.

Today, the Ovadia Law Group has four attorneys, two insurance adjusters, and thirty support staff.

Abraham credits his success to his passion for helping others, especially fighting for the little guy.

Made in the USA
Columbia, SC
21 November 2022

71819224R10057